THE UNIVERSE *ROCKS!*

TO THE PLANETS AND BEYOND

RAMAN PRINJA

To Kamini, Vikas and Sachin

Editorial and Design: Windmill Books Ltd.
Illustrator (activities): Geraint Ford/The Art Agency

Copyright © QED Publishing 2012

First published in the UK in 2012 by
QED Publishing
A Quarto Group company
230 City Road
London EC1V 2TT

www.qed-publishing.co.uk

A catalogue record for this book is available from the British Library.

ISBN 978 1 84835 884 3

Printed in China

Picture credits (t=top, b=bottom, l=left, c=centre, fc=front cover)
  Corbis: Mike Agliol 11br; ESA: 28-29; istockphoto: 1b; NASA: 10bl, 16bl, 21tr, 22bl, 28-
    29, Apollo Gallery 11tr, ESA G Bacon (STScI) 1t, GRIN 2-3, 26-27, Hubble Site 22-
    23, JPL 1tl, 4-5, 4l, 7t, 9tr, 14-15t, 14bl, 15b, 17tr, 19t, 20-21, 31, 32, JPL - Caltech/T.
    Pyle 6-7, 23r; Science Photolibrary: Detlev Van Ravensway 10-11; Shutter-
    stock: 24bl, Marcel Clemens 5t, Elenaphotos 21 16-17, RZ Design 13tr; Guan
    Kehng Toh 24-25, Rick Whitacre 25br,
    *We have made every attempt to contact the copyright holder. If anyone
    has any information please contact smortimer@windmillbooks.co.uk*

    Website information is correct at time of going to press. However,
    the publishers cannot accept liability for any information or links
    found on any Internet sites, including third-party websites.

    In preparation of this book, all due care has been exercised with
    regard to the activities and advice depicted. The publishers regret
    that they can accept no liability for any loss or injury sustained.

Words in **bold**
are explained in
the glossary on
page 31

What is a light-year?

Distances in space are measured in light-years.
A light-year is the distance that light travels in one year.
• In one second light travels 300,000 kilometres
    – or seven times around Earth.
• In one minute light travels 18 million kilometres
    – or to the Moon and back 50 times.
• In one year light travels 9,000 billion kilometres
    – or one light-year.

CONTENTS

TOUR OF THE SOLAR SYSTEM

Our Solar System is made up of a star we call the Sun, eight planets, many dwarf planets, over a hundred moons, millions of rocky asteroids and billions of icy comets.

In this book we will go on a fantastic tour of the Solar System. Our travels will take us from bubbling hot gas on the Sun to **volcanoes** erupting ice and steam on the moons of the outer planets. We will explore the magnificent rings of Saturn and hunt for water beyond Earth.

The Sun

Venus

Mars

Mercury

Earth

Jupiter

Eight worlds

Our Solar System is home to eight planets, the largest objects that orbit the Sun. In order of distance from the Sun they are Mercury, Venus, Earth, Mars, Jupiter, Saturn, Uranus and Neptune.

MERCURY Super-hot during the day, but freezing at night.

VENUS At 450 degrees Celsius this is the hottest planet of them all.

EARTH Our home is the only known planet where life exists. Oceans of liquid water exist on the surface.

Comet

Leftovers

Besides planets there are also smaller objects in the Solar System. There are asteroids made of rock and iron, mostly found between Mars and Jupiter. There are also billions of comets made of rock and ice. As a comet gets close to the Sun, the frozen gases heat up and make huge tails that flow behind the comet.

Saturn

Uranus

Neptune

MARS The red planet has huge mountains and deep canyons, The red colour comes from dust that covers the surface. Mars once had rivers and streams like Earth.

JUPITER This is a giant gas planet – the largest of all – but it has no solid surface to stand on. More than 40 moons circle around Jupiter; some of them are bigger than Mercury.

SATURN All the giant gas planets have rings around them, but none are as beautiful and grand as Saturn's rings.

URANUS Cold methane gas gives Uranus a lovely blue-green colour.

NEPTUNE The farthest planet from the Sun, this gas planet gets very cold.

HOW THE PLANETS WERE MADE

The planets, moons, asteroids and comets were made from gas and dust that was left over after the Sun had formed.

The Sun was made about 5 billion years ago out of a giant cloud of gas and dust. **Gravity** slowly crushed the gas into a large ball that became fiercely hot. The material not used formed a disc around the newly born star. Over millions of years specks of dust joined into clumps, which then stuck together to form rocks. The rocks crashed together, very slowly growing into the planets.

Spinning disc of dust

The Sun

Small rocks grew from billions of specks of dust that bashed into each other and stuck together. These are called asteroids.

Round the Sun

The Sun spins because the cloud it formed from was also spinning. The planets move in the same direction as the star, circling it in paths called **orbits**. Mercury takes just 88 days to complete one lap around the Sun. The Earth takes 365 days and we call this a **year**. Distant Neptune takes 60,100 days (165 Earth years).

| Mercury | Venus | Earth | Mars | Jupiter | Saturn | Uranus | Neptune |

Spinning tops

The planets also turn like spinning tops. The Earth spins around once in 24 hours and we call this a **day**. Venus spins more slowly – and in the other direction – taking 243 Earth days to turn once. But a day on Jupiter is very short. The giant planet spins around in just 10 hours!

Outer planets are mainly gas, although some have cores made of ice and rock.

Rocks inside and gas outside

Close to the Sun where the **temperature** is higher, only small rocky planets formed – Mercury, Venus, Earth and Mars. Farther away from the Sun in the outer Solar System, it was much colder and icy material gathered there.

The giant planets Jupiter, Saturn, Uranus and Neptune form the outer Solar System. They were big enough to trap lots of gas and make huge, thick **atmospheres**.

TOILET-PAPER SOLAR SYSTEM

The planets in our Solar System are separated by enormous distances.

You will need:

* A regular roll of toilet paper (usually more than 200 sheets)
* A large room (or outside space)
* A felt-tipped pen

TRY DOING THIS...

Here is a simple activity to help you understand just how huge the Solar System is.

What's going on?

Earth is nearly 150 million kilometres away from the Sun, and Jupiter is more than 600 million kilometres from the Earth. The farthest planet, Neptune, is about 5 billion kilometres from the Sun. These huge distances are hard for us to imagine. In this activity you can understand the spacing between planets using a scale made from toilet paper.

1 Mark a dot in the middle of the first sheet of the roll. Label this dot the Sun.

2 You can now start to roll out the sheets slowly, taking care not to rip the paper.

Unroll until you have 90 sheets

SUN

3 Mark the positions and names of the rest of the planets along the unwinding roll, using the numbers in this table:

Planets	Sheets (after first sheet)
Mercury	1
Venus	2
Earth	3
Mars	4.5
Jupiter	15.5
Saturn	29
Uranus	57
Neptune	90

SUN · MERCURY · VENUS · EARTH · MARS

4 Now walk along the toilet roll Solar System. Notice how the first four rocky planets are much closer to the Sun than the giant gas planets. In this scale model you would have to roll out 2 million sheets to mark on the next nearest star!

SUN MERCURY VENUS EARTH MARS

In our scale model the length of one sheet of square toilet paper is equal to 50 million kilometres.

...WHAT DID YOU LEARN?

In this activity we have learnt about the different spacing of the paths or orbits of the planets as they go around the Sun. You can try other scale models to explore the different sizes of the planets themselves. For example, imagine the giant planet Jupiter was the size of a basketball. On this very reduced scale, Earth would be the size of a small marble!

FOLLOW THE WATER

Water is very important to us because it makes life on Earth possible.

Living things need water to survive and almost three-quarters of our planet is covered in liquid water as oceans, rivers and lakes. Scientists exploring the Solar System have found water on distant moons and planets. These discoveries are even making people wonder whether simple life-forms, such as **bacteria**, may also be present somewhere else in the Solar System.

Europa is covered in cracks, where the ice is being broken by the movement of water beneath the surface.

Europa

Beneath icy moons

A spacecraft called Galileo took close-up pictures of Europa, one of Jupiter's moons. The pictures showed that Europa had water below its frozen surface. Scientists think there could be an ocean 100 kilometres deep hidden beneath the surface. No one knows if life-forms such as bacteria exist in this dark ocean.

In deep craters

Spacecraft sent to orbit Earth's Moon have discovered water ice in the Moon's deep craters. The craters were formed a long time ago when comets and asteroids crashed into the Moon. Parts of some craters always remain in shadow, and are very cold at the bottom. The water in the craters does not form pools or lakes. It is small icy lumps that are mixed with the dust. Water ice has even been found in cold craters on Mercury!

Moon

Comets crash with a big explosion but some of the water they carry freezes back into ice.

Delivered by comets

Comets are the water bearers of the Solar System. A lot of water was carried by comets, which are made from 'dirty snow'. Billions of years ago the comets crashed into the planets and moons, making craters and dropping icy material.

ERUPTING VOLCANO

The surfaces of Earth, Mars and some moons are shaped by volcanoes that spread lots of liquid rock called lava.

TRY DOING THIS...

In this activity, make a mini volcano that has lava made from bubbles instead of red-hot liquid rock.

It's gonna blow!

The Earth still has many active volcanoes on it today, including some fiery ones on the islands of Hawaii in the Pacific Ocean. Mars has not had any active volcanoes for millions of years, but it does have the largest volcanic mountain in the Solar System. Known as Olympus Mons, this mountain on Mars is three times taller than Mount Everest on Earth.

You will need:

* An empty 500-millilitre plastic water bottle
* Large baking tray
* Heap of soil
* A few drops of red food colouring
* 225 millilitres of vinegar in a jug
* 15 millilitres of bicarbonate of soda
* A tablespoon

1 Place the empty water bottle in the middle of the baking tray. Remove the cap from the bottle.

2 Place soil firmly around the bottle to make a mountain shape. Make sure you don't cover the top of the bottle.

3 Add a few drops of red colouring to the vinegar. This will make your version of fiery lava.

4 Pour the bicarbonate of soda into the bottle using the spoon.

Lava cools down once it comes to the surface, forming a new layer of rock.

5 Now pour the red-coloured vinegar into the bottle and watch what happens! Red foam will rise up out of the bottle and run down the sides of the soil mountain. You've made an erupting volcano!

...WHAT DID YOU LEARN?

When you mixed the vinegar and baking soda in the bottle, they reacted together to make a gas called carbon dioxide. The gas builds up inside the bottle until it forces its way out through the top. Beneath the Earth's crust, magma, a mixture of rock and gases, sometimes does the same thing. It rises up through cracks in rocks and bursts out as lava.

13

ICY VOLCANOES

There are some fantastic wonders in the Solar System and one of the best is volcanoes that blast out ice!

On Earth we see fire and lava pouring from active volcanoes such as Mount Etna in Sicily or on the islands of Hawaii. In the distant Solar System the moons of the giant planets are also covered in volcanoes. But these strange mountains spray out icy rock rather than hot melted rock.

Triton is a dwarf planet that was pulled into Neptune's orbit when the Solar System was young.

Triton

Frozen Triton

One of the coldest places in the Solar System is a moon of Neptune called Triton. The temperature on its surface is -235 degrees Celsius. There are high ridges and deep valleys all over it. A spacecraft called *Voyager 2* flew past Triton and took pictures of active volcanoes. Frozen material was seen rising eight kilometres above Triton's surface. The sprays of fresh ice keep Triton looking white.

Welcome to Enceladus

Enceladus is one of Saturn's 53 known moons. It is only 520 kilometres across and is the eighth furthest moon from the giant planet. The *Cassini* spacecraft has taken a close look at Enceladus. The moon has a bright surface covered by fresh, clean ice. Fountains of water ice blast above the surface. The icy eruptions rise up thousands of kilometres.

Titan's mountains

Titan is the largest moon of Saturn. A The *Cassini* spacecraft made maps of its surface. The maps show an ice volcano 1500 metres high. The water and **ammonia** ice thrown up by this volcano may have helped Titan build up a thick atmosphere around it.

SATURN IN THE SPOTLIGHT

Saturn is one of the most beautiful planets in the Solar System, with its magnificent rings and weird moons.

Saturn is the second largest planet in the Solar System. You could fit nearly 750 Earths inside Saturn! But although Saturn is large, it is mostly made of hydrogen and helium gases. If you could put Saturn in a big enough tank of water, it would float at the top!

Astronomers think Saturn's rings may have been made from a shattered icy moon.

Titan's lakes

Saturn's largest moon, Titan, is the only moon in the Solar System to have a thick atmosphere. Titan is a weird place that has lakes and rivers of oil. The atmosphere is made mainly of nitrogen gas. Scientists are studying Titan because they think it can teach us a lot about how life started on our planet Earth.

Imaginary view of Titan

Storms brewing

There are many raging storms and fierce winds blowing on Saturn. **Hurricanes** at its north pole can be 14,000 kilometres long. There are also lightning storms that last up to six months. They fire bolts of energy that are 10,000 times more powerful than those found on Earth. Near Saturn's **equator**, the speeds of the winds can reach 1,800 kilometres per hour, while the strongest hurricanes on Earth blow at 400 kilometres per hour.

Saturn

Lord of the Rings

All four giant gas planets – Jupiter, Saturn, Uranus and Neptune – have rings around them. But none are as large, bright and beautiful as those of Saturn. The *Cassini* spacecraft beamed back fantastic pictures of Saturn's rings to Earth. The rings are made up of billions of pieces of ice. The frozen bands include tiny ice grains as well as lumps the size of mountains. End-to-end, Saturn's rings stretch 280,000 kilometres. That is three-quarters of the distance from the Earth to the Moon.

CD SATURN

Among the most majestic sights in space are the amazing rings of the gas planet Saturn.

You will need:

* An unwanted CD
* Gold and silver glitter
* Small polystyrene ball (about 5 centimetres across)
* Brush-on glue
* Wooden toothpicks
* Scissors
* Paper clip

Distinctive shape

No other planet looks like Saturn. Even early **astronomers** who looked at it with simple telescopes could see the rings, which stretch out either side. In this activity you can make your own version of the ringed planet.

1 The CD will be used as the rings of Saturn. On one side of the CD use the brush to carefully spread some glue. Avoid the centre part of the CD.

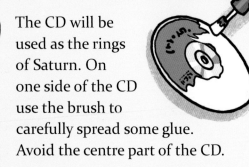

2 Sprinkle the silver and gold glitter on the wet glue and let it dry fully.

3 Ask an adult to cut the polystyrene ball in half. A sharp knife may be needed for this.

Ask an adult to help.

4 Stick one toothpick into the flat side of each half of the ball.

The real Saturn is covered in bands of clouds. Its rings make it twice as wide.

7 You should now have a joined-up ball, with a CD going through its middle. Open the paper clip so it is straight at one end with a hook at the other. Push the straight end of the paper clip into the ball, about 1 centimetre away from the top. This will make your model Saturn tilt when you hang it.

5 Holding the cut half of the ball, using the toothpick as a handle, apply glue to the ball. Sprinkle with glitter. Repeat for the second half and leave both to dry.

8 Attach string to the paper clip hook and hang up your model Saturn!

6 Place one half of the ball on the CD, with the toothpick passing through the hole on the CD. Place the other half of the ball on the other side of the CD. Push both halves of the ball onto the toothpick.

...WHAT DID YOU LEARN?

Does your CD Saturn look the same however you look at it? As Saturn and Earth move, our view of the rings changes. Sometimes they appear very wide, but at other times they are almost impossible to see.

PLUTO AND THE DWARFS

When it was discovered in 1930, Pluto became the ninth and most distant planet of the Solar System.

In 2006, astronomers decided that Pluto was too unusual to be called a normal planet. Pluto has since become known as a dwarf planet, and there are many other dwarf planets in the Solar System. Dwarf planets are different from normal planets because they are small and their path around the Sun is not always clear of other bodies. Astronomers think there may be hundreds of other dwarf planets still to find.

Little worlds

Pluto is a very cold and icy place. Its orbit takes it so far from the Sun that the temperature on its surface can drop to -230 degrees Celsius. Pluto is so cold that its atmosphere can freeze. The largest known dwarf planet is called Eris. It is even further from the Sun than Pluto.

Pluto has three moons, Charon and tiny Nix and Hydra. This is an imaginary view of Pluto from the surface of Nix.

Let's go there

In January 2006, NASA launched a spacecraft on a long journey to Pluto. The mission is called *New Horizons*. After a 5-billion-kilometre journey, the spacecraft will reach Pluto in 2015. *New Horizons* will send back the first ever close-up images of Pluto. It will also study other icy objects and perhaps find new dwarf planets.

New Horizons probe

From Earth, Pluto is too far away to see without a very large telescope. Even then it appears as a fuzzy ball.

Pluto's moon Charon is about a third of the size of the dwarf planet.

What's in a name?

Pluto was named after the Roman god of the underworld. Venetia Burney, an 11-year-old English girl, suggested the name to her grandfather in 1930, and he passed it on to astronomers at the Lowell Observatory. All the planets (apart from Earth) are named after ancient gods. Mercury was named after the messenger of the gods, Venus after the Roman goddess of love and Jupiter after the king of gods.

PLANETS AROUND OTHER STARS

Astronomers have discovered that other stars also have planets orbiting around them.

Our Sun is not the only star with a system of planets and moons. Planets that orbit other stars are called **exoplanets**. Astronomers have so far discovered more than 600 exoplanets around distant stars. There could be billions of exoplanets in our **Galaxy** alone.

This artist's view shows the atmosphere of a hot exoplanet burning off because it is very close to its star.

Super-Earths

Astronomers are using very powerful telescopes to find small Earth-like exoplanets. They have found many that are likely to be rocky worlds. These are called super-Earths because they are bigger than Earth and 5 to 10 times heavier.

Hot Jupiters

Many of the exoplanets found so far are giant gas planets, like Jupiter or Saturn. But while Jupiter and Saturn orbit far away from the Sun, most of these exoplanets are much closer to their star. It's like imagining Jupiter orbiting closer to the Sun than Mercury does! These giant gas exoplanets are sometimes called hot Jupiters.

Some exoplanet systems have two stars at the centre. The planets orbit them both.

Other star systems

Just like our Sun, many other stars also have planets going around them. Experts think perhaps a half of all stars have a planet system. An example of a exoplanet system is called Kepler-11. This star is 2000 light-years away from Earth and has at least six planets. Most of these planets are the size of Uranus and Neptune. Five of the planets in Kepler-11 orbit closer to their star than Mercury does around the Sun.

LIFE BEYOND EARTH

There is water under the surfaces of the moons of Jupiter. Could there also be life?

Hundreds of new planets have been found orbiting around other stars. These exciting discoveries make us wonder whether life-forms may also exist on other planets and moons in space.

Goldilocks planets

Astronomers are looking for exoplanets similar to Earth where life could exist. These exoplanets need to be the right distance from the Sun. Just like Goldilock's porridge, the planet must not be too hot or too cold. The Earth-like exoplanets must be at the right temperature so that oceans of liquid water can exist. Life is more likely to start on a warm, wet planet.

Life as we know it

Earth's living things survive in some very harsh places. For example, we find life in dark oceans where sunlight never shines. Even in baking hot deserts simple life forms such as bacteria can still survive. These environments are not so different from conditions in dry valleys on Mars or deep oceans of Jupiter's moon Europa. For life to exist on another planet it will need liquid water, and chemical **elements** such as carbon.

The Milky Way

Lots of Earths?

There are 200 billion stars in our galaxy, the Milky Way, and billions of these stars are like the Sun. One out of five of the Sun-like stars could have Earth-like planets. This means there could be almost a billion Earth-like planets just in our galaxy. That's a lot of planets where life may have started!

PAPER-CUP SUNDIAL

People have used sundials since ancient times to tell the time of day. Sundials use the changing shadow cast by the Sun as it rises and sets.

TRY DOING THIS...

In this activity you can make your own simple sundial to tell the time of day.

You will need:

* Large paper cup with a lid that has a hole for a straw
* Stiff straw (not a bendy one)
* Watch or clock
* Sharp pencil
* Sticky tape
* Sand or stones
* A compass that points to North

1 Make a hole in the side of the cup using the pencil. Make sure it is about 5 centimetres down from the top of the cup. The hole should be wide enough for a straw to pass through it.

5 cm

2 Half fill the cup with stones or sand to weigh it down. Put the lid on the cup.

Shadow length

When the Sun is high overhead, the shadows are at their shortest. The shadows are much longer in the early morning or late afternoon.

5 Find a place outside where the sunlight falls most of the day. Use a compass to point the straw to the North. At 10 a.m. mark a line on the lid to show where the shadow of the straw falls.

N.

S.

3 Push the straight straw through the hole in the lid and also through the hole in the side of the cup. The straw should stick up about 5 centimetres above the lid.

6 Repeat this every hour until 4 p.m. So you should have marked all the positions the shadow of the straw moved through each hour from 10 a.m. to 4 p.m., and written down the hours on the lid. The next sunny day, go back to the same place and read the time with your sundial.

4 Tape the other end of the straw onto the cup. Now you are ready to use your sundial.

...WHAT DID YOU LEARN?

The shadows move on the sundial because the Sun appears to move across the sky. But the Sun isn't really moving. It appears to move because the Earth is spinning around every 24 hours.

The Sun is always shining somewhere on Earth, even when it is night where you are.

REALLY COOL STUFF ABOUT PLANETS

Every planet is a world of its own, with many remarkable features that are literally out of this world!

Do comets crash into the Sun?

The Sun is a massive object with very strong gravity. Sometimes comets swinging in from the outer parts of the solar system come too close to the Sun and get trapped by the enormous pull of the Sun's gravity. The comets can end up crashing into the Sun!

Can you walk on asteroids?

Asteroids are mostly very small and so their gravity is very weak. An astronaut standing on an asteroid would weigh very little. This makes taking steps on the asteroid very difficult and the astronaut would mostly float on the surface.

Is it raining diamonds on Neptune?

Neptune has a lot of methane gas in its huge atmosphere. Scientists think that the temperature and force of the gas inside Neptune is so high that the methane can turn into diamonds! Once the diamonds are made they would fall like raindrops toward the centre of the planet.

Did something from space kill the dinosaurs?

Some scientists think that most dinosaurs died when a huge asteroid struck Earth about 65 million years ago. The powerful crash made giant clouds of dust rise into the air and block out the sunlight for many months. The dust changed the climate and made the dinosaurs die out.

What are Solar flares?

Every now and then small patches on the Sun erupt in flashes, known as flares. These release huge amounts of energy. The largest solar flare can blast billions of tons of superhot gas into space. The amount of energy released in a single flare can be millions of times larger than that of a volcano exploding on Earth.

Why is Uranus on its side?

All planets spin vertically on their axes, apart from Uranus. This spins on its side, like a barrel rolling around the Sun! It could be that massive Earth-sized objects crashed into it billions of years ago and knocked it over!

Will Mars have a ring one day?

One of Mars' two moons is called Phobos. This moon is slowly moving towards the planet. In perhaps 10 million years from now, Phobos will get so close to Mars that the planet's gravity will break the small moon apart. When Phobos shatters the material will form a thin ring around Mars!

Why is there a big red spot on Jupiter?

A hurricane has been raging on Jupiter for more than 400 years! It is called the Great Red Spot because of the way it looks. Almost three Earths could fit side-by-side inside it.

Is there acid rain on Venus?

Clouds on Venus are made of a very nasty acid called sulphuric acid. But Venus is so hot that acid rain never falls to the ground. It evaporates high above the surface.

Is Earth's Moon drifting away?

The distance between the Earth and its Moon has been measured carefully using lasers since astronauts visited the Moon in the 1970s. The measurements show the Moon drifting away from the Earth by 4 centimetres every year!

Top Ten Planet Facts

1. Jupiter is the largest planet in the Solar System. Nearly 1320 Earths would fit inside Jupiter.

2. Saturn has the widest rings of any planet. The span of its rings is only slightly less than the distance between the Earth and Moon.

3. Jupiter is the fastest-spinning planet, turning once in just under ten hours.

4. Venus is the hottest planet, with a surface that can rise to 460 degrees Celsius – hot enough to melt lead!

5. Neptune has the fastest winds in the Solar System, reaching speeds of more than 2000 km per hour.

6. The Solar System's largest moon is Ganymede, which orbits Jupiter and is larger than the planet Mercury.

7. The tallest mountain in the solar system is Olympus Mons on Mars. It is nearly three times higher than Mount Everest on Earth.

8. Venus is the brightest planet we can see in the night sky.

9. Neptune is the coldest planet of our Solar System, with temperatures that can drop to -200 degrees Celsius.

10. There are more active volcanoes and earthquakes on Earth than any other planet in the Solar System.

Websites

Hubble Space Telescope Gallery http://hubblesite.org/gallery

European Space Agency http://www.esa.int

BBC Space http://www.bbc.co.uk/science/space/

NASA http://www.nasa.gov/audience/forkids/kidsclub/flash/index.html

National Geographic Space http://science.nationalgeographic.com/science/space/

Online Star Map http://www.open2.net/science/finalfrontier/planisphere/planisphere_embedded.html

GLOSSARY

ammonia A smelly chemical made from hydrogen and nitrogen.

asteroid A space rock. Most asteroids orbit in a belt between Mars and Jupiter.

astronomer A scientist who studies stars, planets and other objects in space.

atmosphere The gases that surround a planet or moon.

bacteria Tiny life forms, sometimes known as germs.

comet An icy body with an orbit that brings it close to the Sun at regular intervals.

day The amount of time it takes for a planet to spin around once. Earth's day is 24 hours, but Venus's is 243 Earth days!

Earth's crust The shell of rocks that surrounds our planet.

element A pure chemical, such as hydrogen, oxygen, carbon or nitrogen.

equator The imaginary line that divides a planet into a northern and southern half.

exoplanet A planet that orbits a star that is not the Sun.

galaxy Collection of billions of stars held together by gravity.

gravity A force that attracts objects together.

hurricane A powerful storm with strong winds.

light-year The distance travelled by light in one year.

orbit The path that a planet takes around the Sun. Orbits are oval in shape.

temperature A measure of how much heat is inside something.

volcanoes Openings in a planet's surface through which hot liquid rock is thrown up.

year The amount of time it takes for a planet to go around the Sun. Earth's year is 365 days but every other planet's year is different.

INDEX